MEDICI ART BOOKS

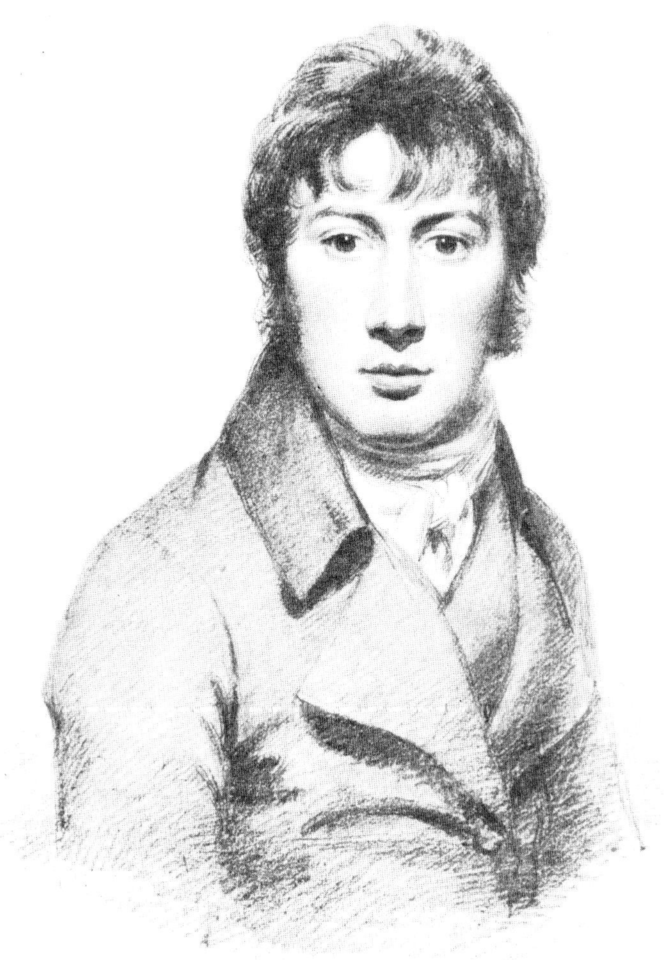

JOHN CONSTABLE

by Edward Allhusen

THE MEDICI SOCIETY LTD
LONDON 1976

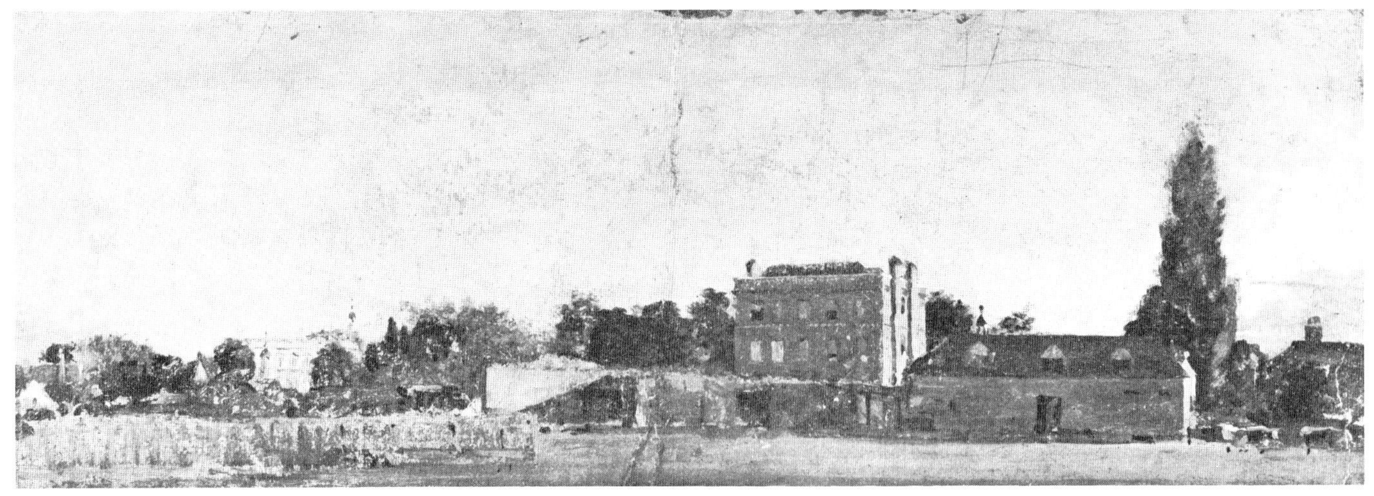

Golding Constable's House, East Bergholt, c.1811. Victoria and Albert Museum, London.

John Constable was born on 11th June 1776 in the reign of King George III. It was a time of great change in England; the Industrial Revolution was gaining momentum and within a month of John's birth America declared independence.

John was the second son of Golding and Anne Constable whose home was at East Bergholt in Suffolk. It was feared that the baby would not live and for this reason his parents arranged for him to be baptised a few hours after his birth. However, he grew into a sturdy child and went to school first at Bergholt and then to Lavenham where the pupils were beaten to such an extent that his parents moved him to the Grammar School at Dedham. Doctor Grimwood, the headmaster at his new school, was a kind man who noticed his pupil's talents and encouraged him to sketch and draw.

Golding Constable was a prosperous miller who held a position of importance in the predominantly agricultural neighbourhood. He had inherited Flatford Mill on the River Stour from an uncle and later expanded his business by purchasing another watermill at Dedham and two windmills at Bergholt. In later life John frequently referred to the happiness of his childhood and this seems to be reflected by the peaceful representation of the countryside around Bergholt which formed the basis of so much of his best-loved work. The house in which he was born, now demolished, was built by his father in 1774 to accommodate his growing family. Constable made many sketches of the impressive three storey, red brick house which stood in thirty-seven acres of land with large gardens, a coach-house and stables (p. 2).

It was Golding's wish that his son John should become a clergyman, but seeing that he showed no inclination for this, it was decided that he should join the milling business and for a year the boy worked hard to learn his father's trade.

He had now grown tall and with his neat appearance became known in the neighbourhood as 'The Handsome Miller'. The experience he gained at this time was to be of great value, for he learnt to observe the skies and winds carefully in order to set the sails of his father's windmills to best advantage. He also acquired an intimate knowledge of the picturesque machinery of the locks and watermills on the River Stour, and his brother Abram later wrote 'When I look at a painting of a mill by John, I see that it will go round, which is not always the case with other artists'. Constable loved the cottages, the woods and the rivers around his home and wrote that 'the trees and the clouds seem to ask me to try and do something like them'. He also studied natural history from a scientific point of view and copied botanical drawings. His favourite book at this time was Gilbert White's *Natural History of Selborne* which he read many times.

At an early age Constable mentioned to his father that his choice of career was that of a painter, but Golding, knowing that few men were able to make a satisfactory living in this way, opposed the idea from the beginning. After this the boy was obliged to paint out of his father's sight and much of his sketching was done in the countryside. When he wished to work indoors he made use of a room in the home of John Dunthorne, a builder and glazier, who lived in the same village. Both Dunthorne and his son, whose name was also John, were accomplished artists and the latter exhibited at the Royal Academy in the six years before his death at the early age of 34.

Constable's mother showed greater foresight than her husband and encouraged her son's drawing. She arranged for him to meet Sir George Beaumont during one of the latter's visits to his mother, who

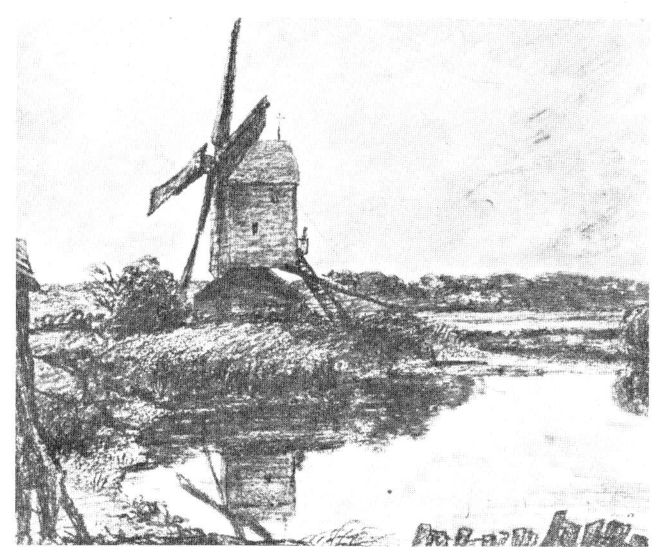

A Mill on the Banks of the River Stour, 1802. Victoria and Albert Museum, London.

also lived at Dedham. Sir George owned a collection of paintings by Rubens, Girtin and Claude and was so fond of Claude's painting *Hagar and the Angel*, which is now in the National Gallery, London, that he often took it with him when he travelled. Constable was shown this painting when Sir George brought it to Dedham and for the first time he was able to study the work of a great master. He learnt much from Claude's technique and considered that the first sight of this painting was one of the major turning points of his life.

Sir George recognised the talents of the young Constable and in 1795 persuaded Golding to allow his son to travel to London. There he met many other artists and was able to copy paintings by Ruysdael, Claude and Wilson, the latter having considerable influence on his earlier work.

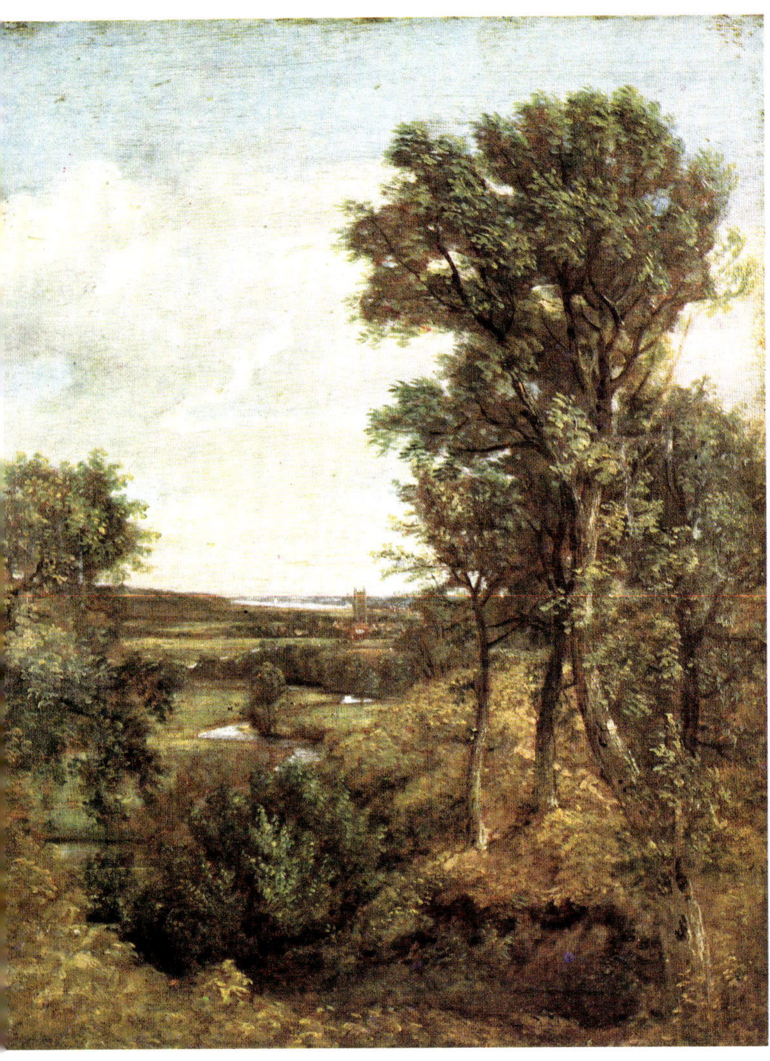

Dedham Vale, 1802. Victoria and Albert Museum, London. This view of the Stour valley and Dedham with its church tower is one of Constable's earliest paintings to have a more finished appearance. He used this small painting, twenty years later, as the basis for a six-foot canvas of the same scene, now in The National Gallery of Scotland.

Constable now divided his time between Bergholt and London, but in 1799 Golding Constable realised that he could no longer ignore his son's desire to become a painter and gave him permission to leave the mill and live permanently in London, paying him a small allowance.

Constable took rooms at 23 Cecil Street near the Strand and enrolled at the Royal Academy Schools. He greatly enjoyed his time there though whenever possible he still left London to sketch and draw in the countryside. Writing to Dunthorne from London he said 'I am come to a determination to make no idle visits this summer. . . . I shall shortly return to Bergholt where I shall make some laborious studies from nature—and I shall endeavour to get a pure and unaffected representation of the scenes that may employ me with respect to colour particularly . . . . drawing I am pretty well master of'.

Constable's first love was always landscape but he was able to supplement his modest income not only by painting portraits from life but also by copying those in the collections of wealthy families. Many members of his family, neighbours and friends also sat to him.

In 1800 and 1801 he sent pictures to the Royal Academy but they were rejected. However, the President, Benjamin West, consoled him with the words 'Don't be disheartened, young man, we shall hear of you again; you must have loved nature very much before you could have painted this.' and, taking up a piece of chalk, transformed the picture with a few deft touches, saying 'Always remember, Sir, that light and shadow never stand still'. This brief lesson had a lasting effect on Constable's work.

The following year, 1802, saw the first of his landscapes accepted by the Academy. In this year also,

West, who was a great friend to all the young students, helped Constable again when he dissuaded him from accepting a post as lecturer at Marlow Military College which, though offering financial security for the first time in his life, would have prevented him from spending as much time in the countryside.

In the same year Constable painted a view of *Dedham Vale* (p. 4) basing the composition on *Hagar and the Angel*, Sir George Beaumont's favourite picture. In it we see both the meandering River Stour and Dedham Church which were to appear in so many of his later works.

Constable did not exhibit at the Royal Academy again until 1805, when another landscape was accepted, and in this year he also painted for Brantham Church the first of his three altarpieces.

In 1806 he commemorated the Battle of Trafalgar with a watercolour which was hung at the Academy that year entitled *His Majesty's Ship Victory in the Battle of Trafalgar between two French Ships of the Line*. Having spent a month at sea in a clipper ship in 1803 and sketched the *Victory* at Chatham at that time, the idea occurred to him when listening to the account of a Suffolk man who had been on board Nelson's flagship during the battle.

Later that year the generosity of an uncle enabled him to travel north to Derbyshire and the Lake District where he found the colours very challenging, though the grandeur of the scenery left him unimpressed. He wrote that he thought it a lonely place and his *A Bridge, Borrowdale* (p. 8) shows what a contrast it must have been to his native Suffolk. On the back of the canvas he wrote 'Borrowdale Oct. 2. 1806—twylight after a very fine day'. It was the farthest he ever travelled from home.

Since childhood Constable had been friendly with

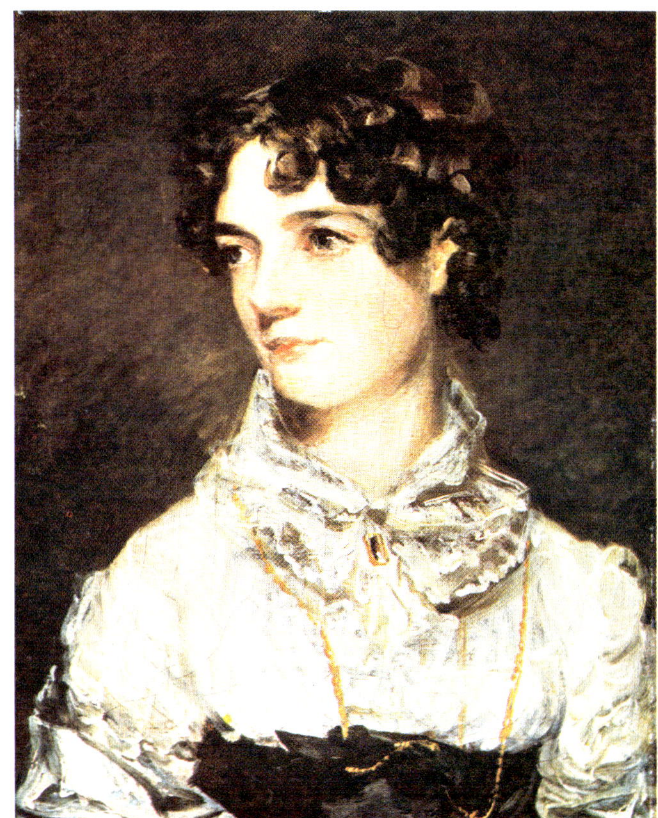

Maria Bicknell (later Mrs Constable), 1816. Tate Gallery, London.

Maria Bicknell, whose father was Solicitor to the Admiralty. They had met when she stayed with her well-to-do grandfather Dr Durand Rhudde, the rector of Bergholt and a chaplain in ordinary to George III. In 1809 they met again and by 1811 they had fallen in love, but when the subject of their marriage was raised, Dr Rhudde, regarding a struggling artist with virtually no income as a most unsuitable partner in marriage for his grand-daughter,

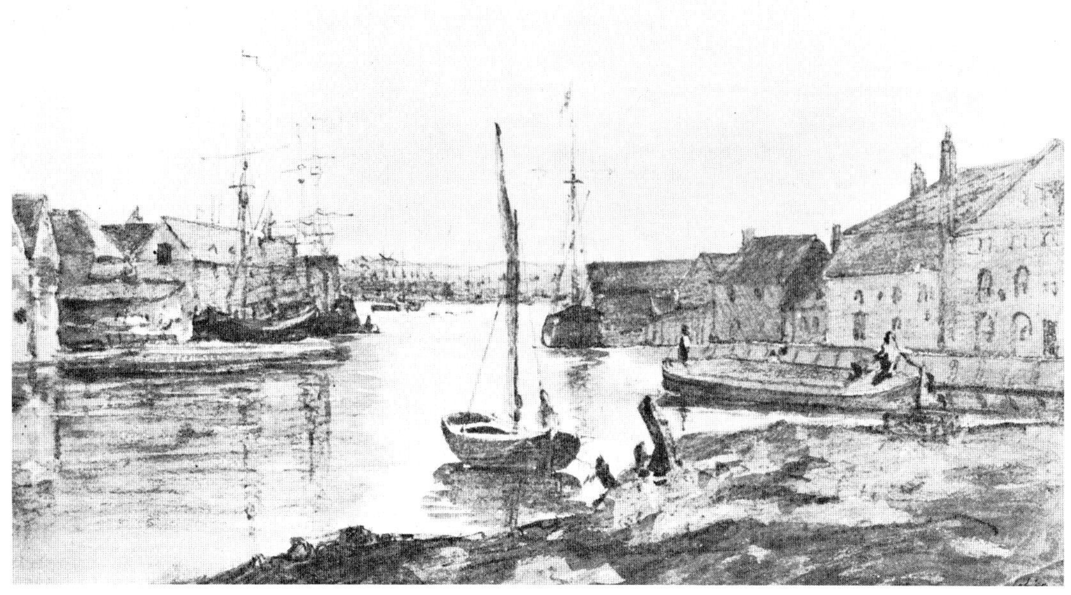

Warehouses and Shipping on the Orwell at Ipswich, 1803. Victoria and Albert Museum, London.

immediately forbade further meetings or correspondence between them and threatened to cut Maria out of his will if she continued to see Constable. His objection was certainly also to the station in life of the Constable family, which in the nineteenth century would have been thought inferior to his own.

In 1811 Constable made the first of his many visits to Dr Fisher, Bishop of Salisbury, an old family friend. Bishop Fisher was extremely generous to Constable and over the years commissioned a number of paintings, the best known of which is *Salisbury Cathedral from the Bishop's Grounds* (p. 16) painted in 1823. Though the Bishop at first criticised the picture, later in the same year he commissioned a smaller version from Constable as a wedding present for his daughter. During his visits to Salisbury Constable became a close friend of the Bishop's chaplain and nephew, John Fisher, who was later to become

Archdeacon of Berkshire. Their friendship lasted until Fisher's death in 1832 and he also bought a number of Constable's paintings. They corresponded frequently and their letters show that Constable greatly valued the help and encouragement that Fisher was able to give him.

Despite the threat of disinheritance, John and Maria continued to correspond for five long years and saw each other as often as possible. During this difficult courtship Constable continued his struggle to establish himself as an artist. His pictures were hung each year at the Royal Academy and in 1810 he obtained another commission for an altarpiece, this time at Nayland (p. 9). In 1814 he applied for election as an Associate of the Royal Academy but failed to get a single vote. The following year, however, he was greatly encouraged when one of the pictures he had shown at the Academy in 1814 was sold to a Mr

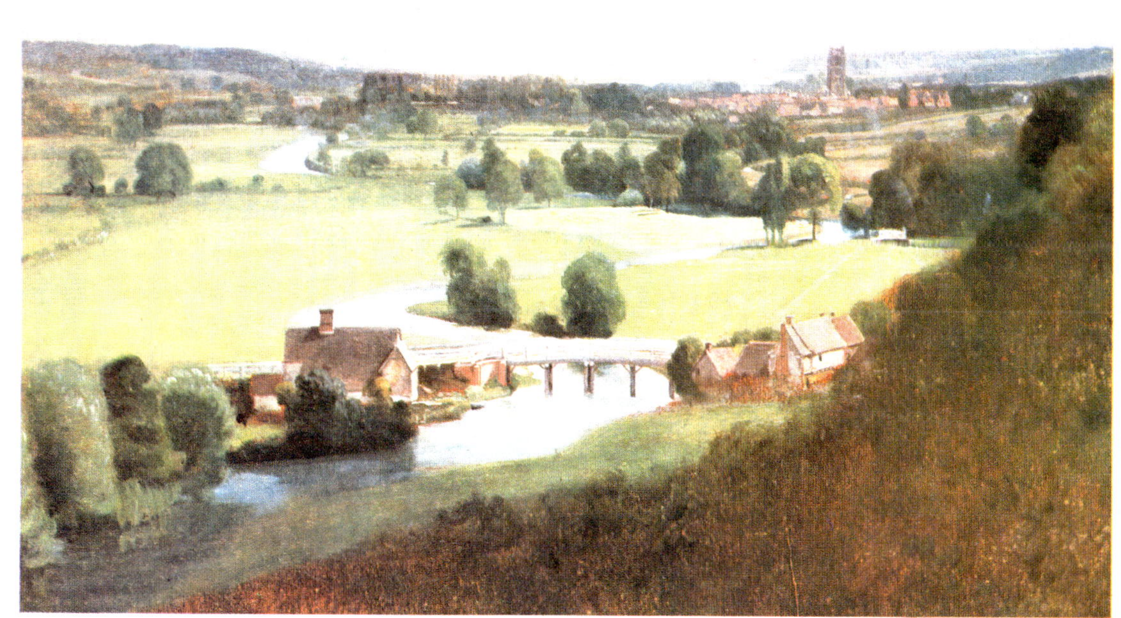

The Valley of the Stour, with Dedham in the distance (detail), c.1805. Victoria and Albert Museum, London.

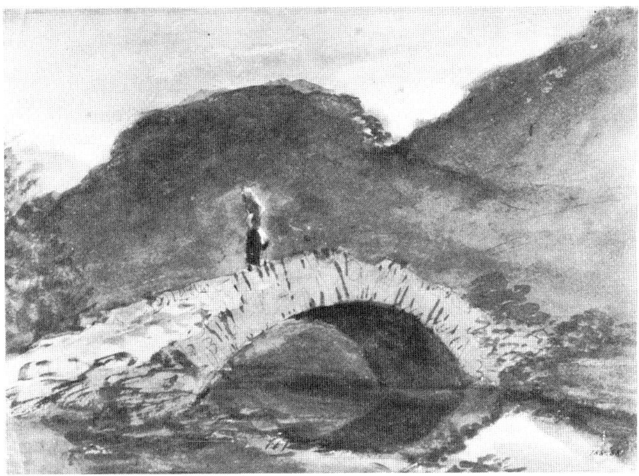

A Bridge, Borrowdale, 1806. Victoria and Albert Museum, London.

Allnutt, who was previously unknown to him. This was the first time that he had sold a landscape to a stranger.

In 1815 he painted *Boat-building near Flatford Mill* (p. 11), the forerunner of the much more highly finished paintings which are now his best-loved works, and it was accepted by the Academy that year. He wrote that the fine weather had enabled him to paint the whole picture out-of-doors, and the work shows how adept Constable had now become at capturing atmosphere on canvas. The haze of the hot summer's day can be seen rising from the riverside meadows and work on the new barge seems to be proceeding at a leisurely pace. Like all his major paintings, this picture was preceded by many preparatory sketches starting with pencil drawings of various details and alternative compositions (p. 11) and working up to an oil sketch the same size as the finished work.

1815 was, however, also a sad year for Constable as his mother, whose encouragement had meant so much, died in the spring. Maria Bicknell's mother also died, three days later, and their similar loss drew John and Maria closer together, but still Dr Rhudde refused to agree to their marriage. Another blow came in the following year when Golding Constable died. Although always opposed to his son's becoming an artist he was an understanding man whose only objection to John's chosen career had been on financial grounds. The two had remained on excellent terms since John's departure from the milling business, and he now inherited a share in the estate.

Happily, however, this change in Constable's circumstances caused Dr Rhudde, now an old man, to give his reluctant consent to his grand-daughter's persistent wishes, and John and Maria were at last married. The ceremony was conducted by John Fisher at St. Martin-in-the-Fields in London on 2nd October 1816. On the doctor's death three years later, the couple were delighted to find that he had left Maria £4,000.

For their honeymoon John and Maria travelled to Osmington in Dorset and stayed with Fisher, who was by then rector there and who had himself been married a few months before. Constable found the cliffs and seas of this coast ideal subjects for his sketchbooks, and some of his finest cloud studies were drawn here on this and their many subsequent visits.

On their return to London, the Constables set up house in Keppel Street, near Russell Square. Now that the strain and uncertainty of his long courtship were over, Constable entered the happiest and most productive period of his life. Almost every year of his marriage saw the completion of another major painting, and the happiness and contentment that Maria brought him shines through his best-loved works.

Flatford Mill (p. 12), the first of these, was painted in 1817, but though it was hung at the Academy in that year it was never sold, and remained in Constable's possession for the rest of his life.

The White Horse, completed two years later, was the first of his canvases to exceed six feet in width. It is another river scene showing a barge horse being ferried across the river at a point where the towpath changes from one bank to the other.

Though it had been Constable's ambition for many years to be elected an Associate of the Royal Academy his paintings of everyday life were such a contrast to the conventional dramatic scenes from the Bible or mythology that he met much opposition. More importance, however, was now being attached to accuracy of light and colour, and in 1819 his achievements in this direction were at last recognised and his ambition fulfilled. At this time he also began to sell more paintings, though he told another artist that as he rarely earned more than £100 in any year he paid no tax since the authorities did not consider this sum a living.

The mill at Stratford, upstream from Dedham, was used for making paper and Constable chose this stretch of the River Stour for his second six-foot painting, which was completed in 1820 and purchased by John Fisher as a present for his lawyer. The small boys fishing in the foreground have earned the painting the alternative title of *The Young Waltonians*, a reference to Isaak Walton's famous book *The Compleat Angler*.

In 1820 he also painted *Dedham Lock and Mill* (p. 13) showing one of his father's mills where he had worked as a boy. In the following year he exhibited a large canvas at the Royal Academy which he simply called *Landscape. Noon*. It was John Fisher who first gave it the name by which it is now so well known when he asked the artist what progress was being made on *The Haywain* (p. 14).

Cont. p.13

Altarpiece, 1810. St. James's Church, Nayland, Suffolk.

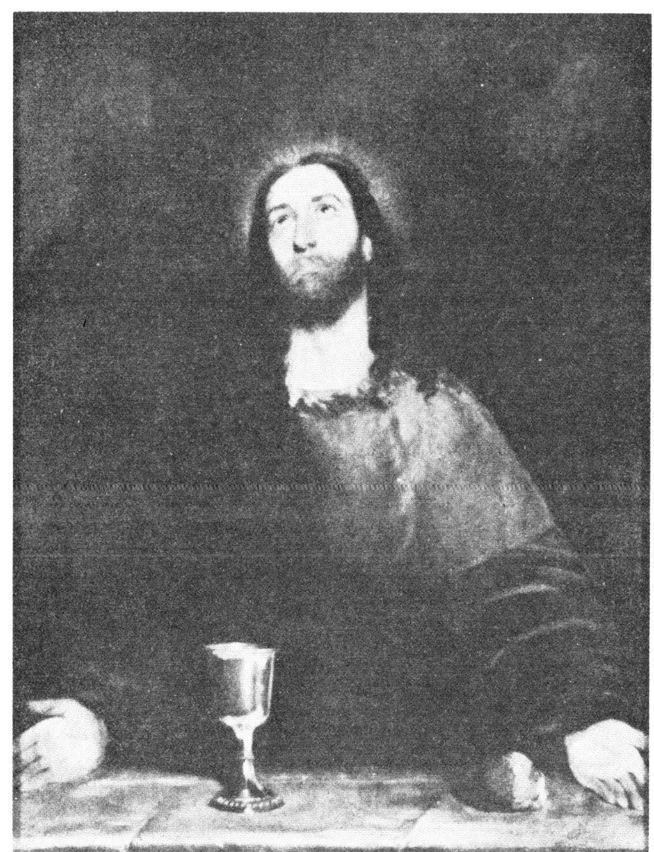

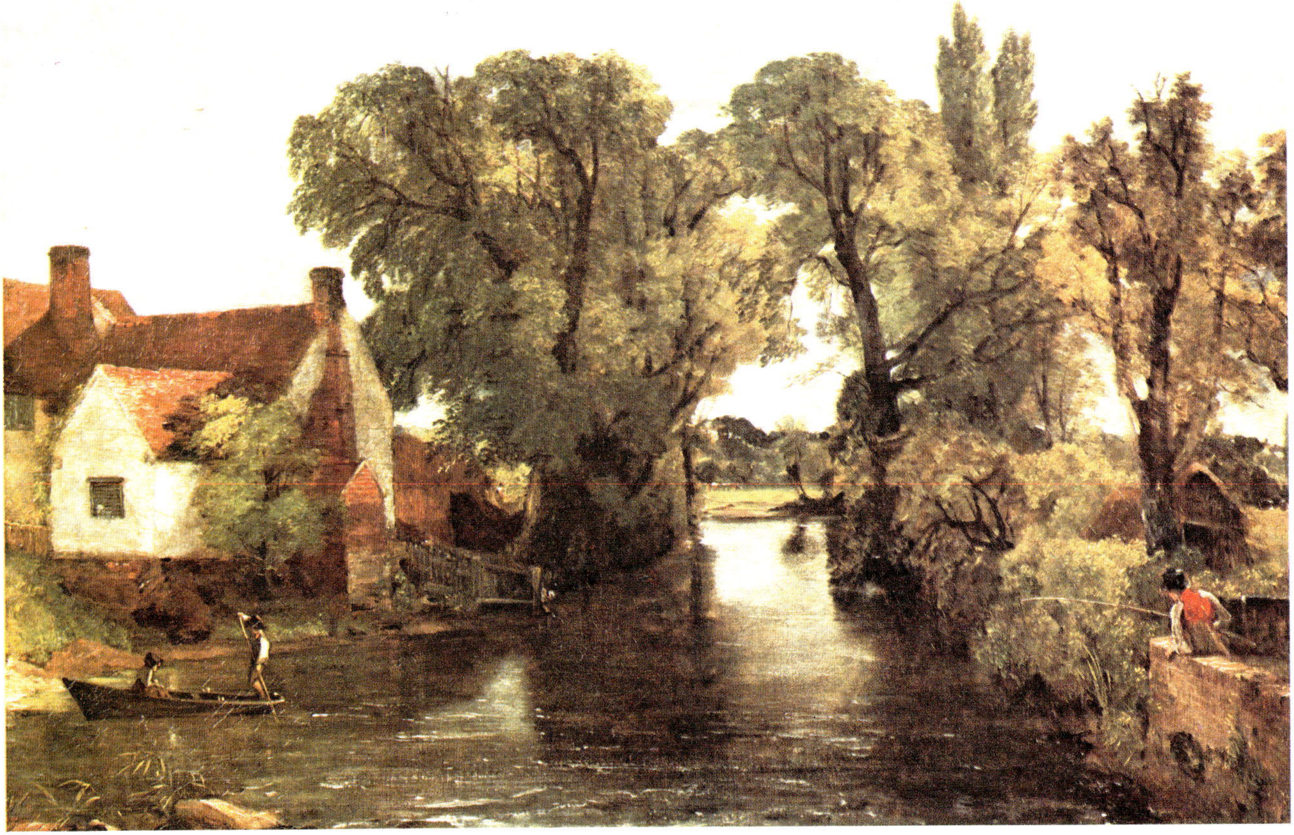

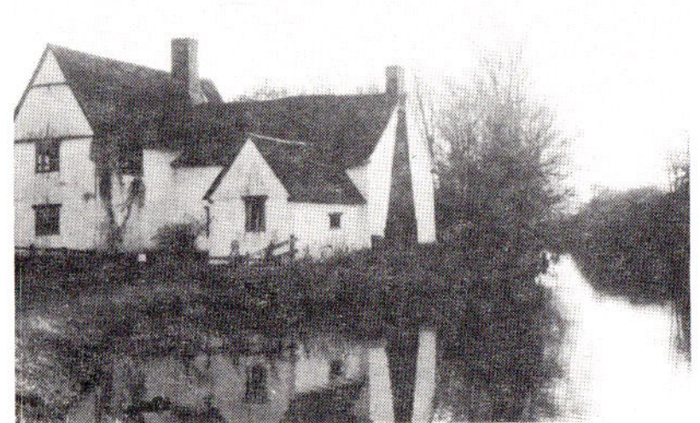

Willy Lott's Cottage as it is today. Photograph, J. Gurney.

The Mill Stream, c. 1814. Ipswich Borough Council.
This painting shows Willy Lott's cottage and the ferry over the mill stream beside Flatford Mill. Painted whilst Constable was uncertain about his future with Maria, the picture provoked a letter of criticism from an uncle urging Constable not to allow his state of mind to interfere with his work.

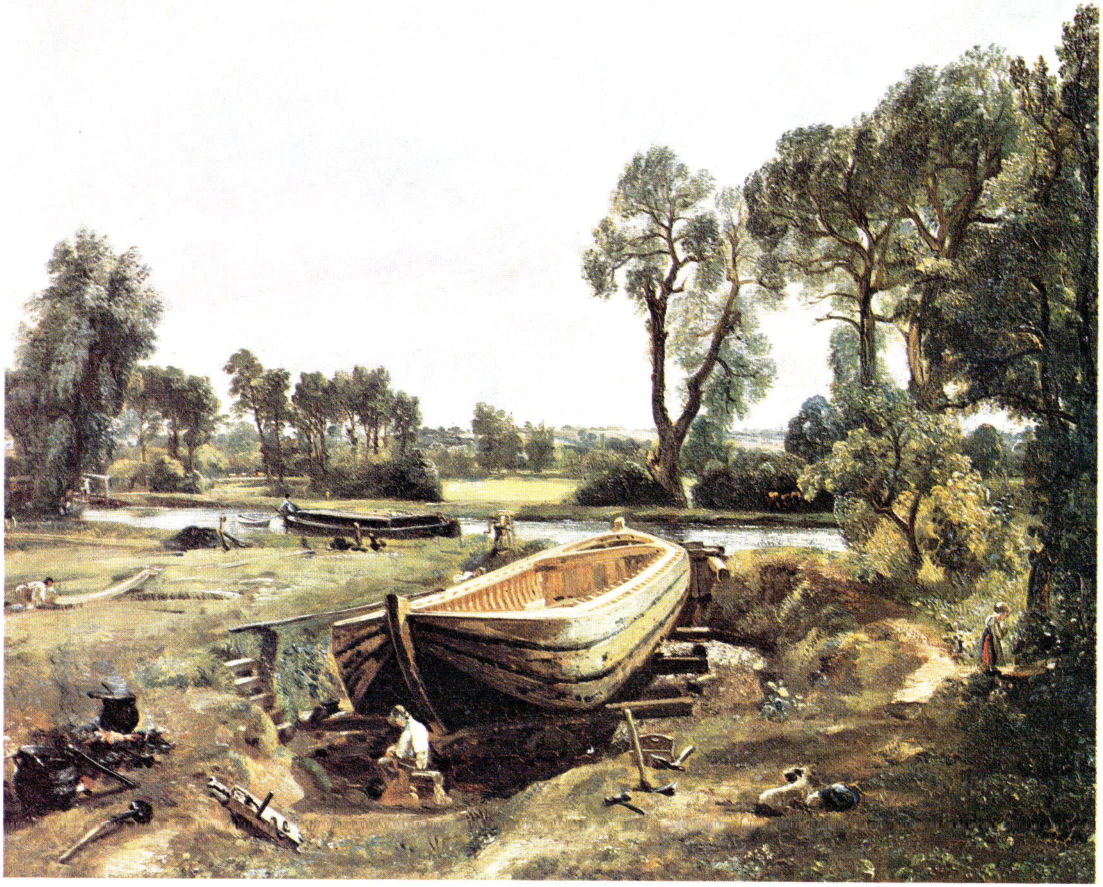

Boat-building near Flatford Mill, 1815. Victoria and Albert Museum, London.
This picture shows Golding Constable's men building a barge in his dock. The tools lying around the barge include adzes, a sledgehammer, a jack and large ladles for handling the pitch being heated in the cauldron for caulking the seams of the boat. In the background timbers are being shaped and a horse is towing another barge upstream towards Dedham. Flatford Lock can be seen amongst the trees on the left. *A View on the Stour near Dedham* (p. 15) was painted from the dock entrance.

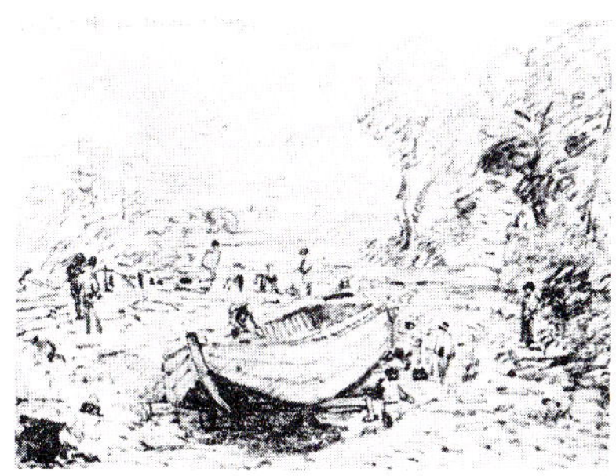

Study for *Boat-building near Flatford Mill*, 1814. Victoria and Albert Museum, London.

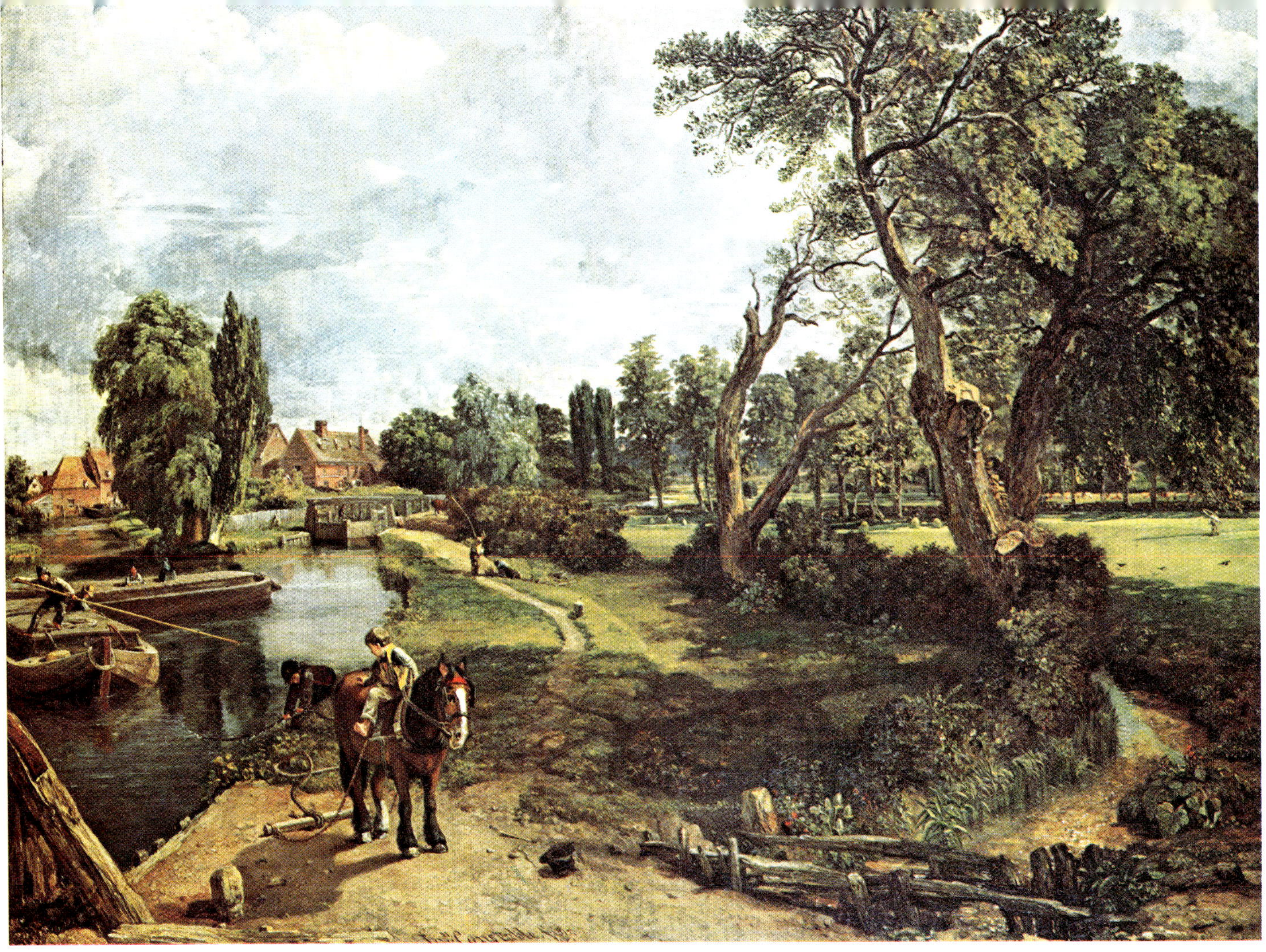

Flatford Mill, 1817. Tate Gallery, London.
Flatford Mill on the River Stour was owned by Constable's father and John worked there as a young man.

The baulk of timber in the foreground is part of the parapet of the foot bridge which can be seen in *A View on the Stour near Dedham* (p. 15). As the towpath does not pass under the bridge, the barge horse is being unharnessed so that the boat can be 'poled' under the bridge. The small boy astride the horse has dropped his hat and whip and looks round waiting eagerly for the tow rope to be untied so that he can ride the short distance down the towpath.

In the background, the mill stream leaves the main course of the river beside the lock which appears also in *A Boat Passing a Lock* (p. 19). The trees are bathed in sunshine and the blue sky with gentle billowing clouds show that it is the height of summer.

A comparison of *The Haywain* with *The Mill Stream* (p. 10), painted seven years before, when his future with Maria was still in doubt, shows clearly Constable's new mood. The overcast sky and sombre shadows of the earlier painting give way to the sparkling colour and sunny atmosphere of the same scene through new eyes.

The Haywain had a good reception at the Royal Academy in 1821, but remained unsold until three years later when a dealer named Arrowsmith bought it together with *A View on the Stour near Dedham* (p. 15) and a small picture of Yarmouth for £250. He exhibited the paintings at the Salon in Paris where—less than a decade after Waterloo—they were received with great acclaim and Constable was awarded two gold medals by the King of France. His fresh approach greatly impressed French artists and Delacroix is said to have completely revised one of his own paintings after seeing *The Haywain*.

The dealers in Paris placed orders for many more paintings and before long twenty-five had been exhibited in France. This sudden interest in his

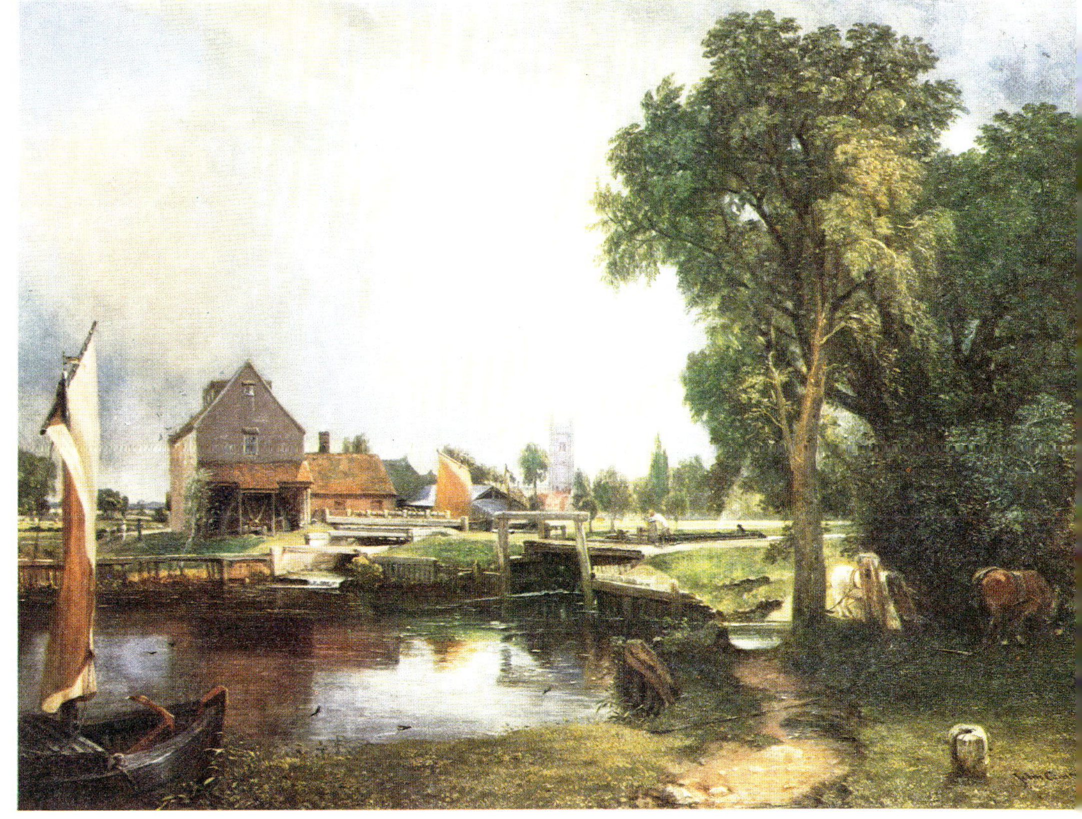

Dedham Lock and Mill, 1820. Victoria and Albert Museum, London.
This painting is a study of life on the River Stour beside Dedham Mill. In the foreground a barge is moored waiting to move upstream; the mast will have to be unstepped before it can do so to enable it to pass under the beam and footbridge across the entrance to the lock. A second barge has entered the lock from above and the boatman can be seen opening the sluice to lower the level of the water. The horses of both barges, still in harness, are grazing under the trees. Behind the lock more barges can be seen, perhaps loading flour from the mill. The sluices to the left of the lock regulate the flow of water under the mill wheel which can be seen turning beyond. In the background is the town of Dedham with its impressive church tower.

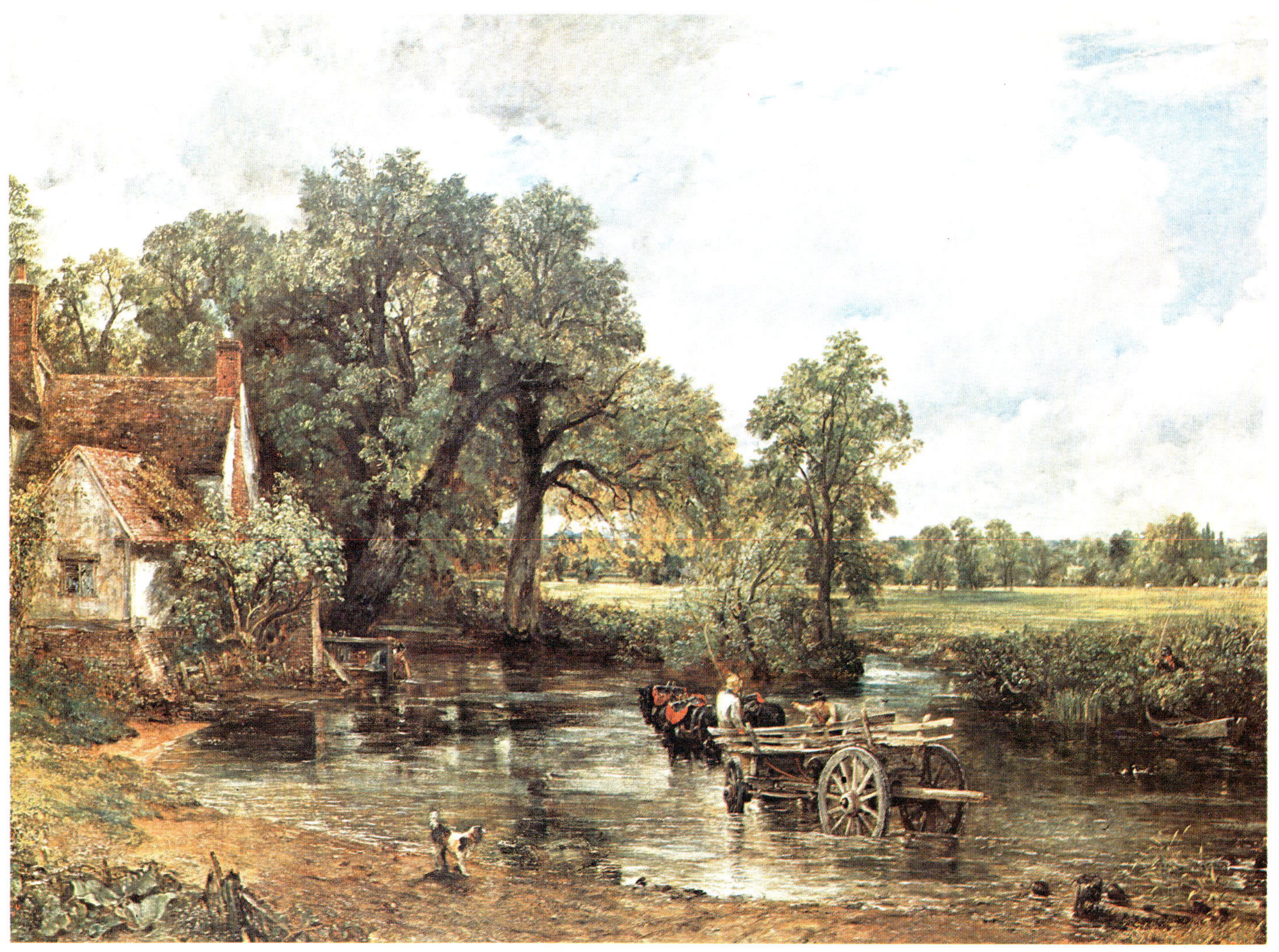

The Haywain, 1821. National Gallery, London.

This stretch of water is beside Flatford Mill. The cottage on the left, which appears in many of Constable's paintings, was the home of Willy Lott who lived there for over eighty years. *The Mill Stream* (p. 10) is a slightly different view of it and the photograph on the same page shows it almost unchanged today.

Beside the cottage a woman is washing clothes in the river and among the bushes on the far bank a man can be seen fishing beside his boat. The horses have finished drinking and are backing the cart to turn out of the water. The wheel tracks on the ground where the dog is walking show this to be a favourite place for teams of work horses to water.

The carefully painted sunlit trees and delicate clouds strongly convey the atmosphere of mid-summer.

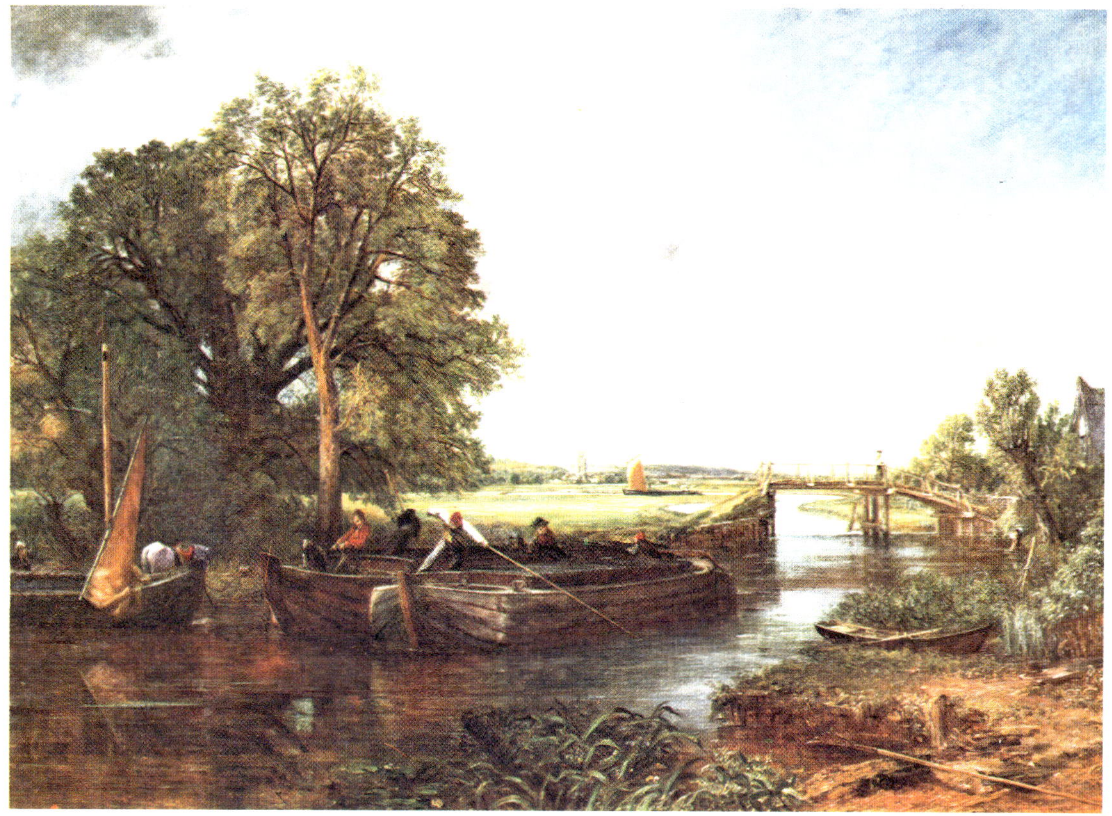

A View on the Stour near Dedham, 1822. Henry E. Huntingdon Library and Art Gallery, San Marino, California.

paintings greatly improved his income and he asked the younger John Dunthorne to come to London as his assistant to help with the work. A talented craftsman and a keen amateur astronomer, making and repairing his own telescopes, Dunthorne was himself an accomplished artist and he helped Constable by preparing canvases and drawing outlines for him.

Constable's major work in 1822 was *A View on the Stour near Dedham* (p. 15), showing the river close to Flatford Mill with Dedham in the background. This is another sunny scene of life on the river with bargemen at work and a lady out for a walk.

Much of 1823 was spent on the two versions of *Salisbury Cathedral from the Bishop's Grounds* referred to earlier. The picture illustrated on page 16 was hung at the Academy that year.

At about this time Maria's health was beginning to show signs of the consumption which was eventually

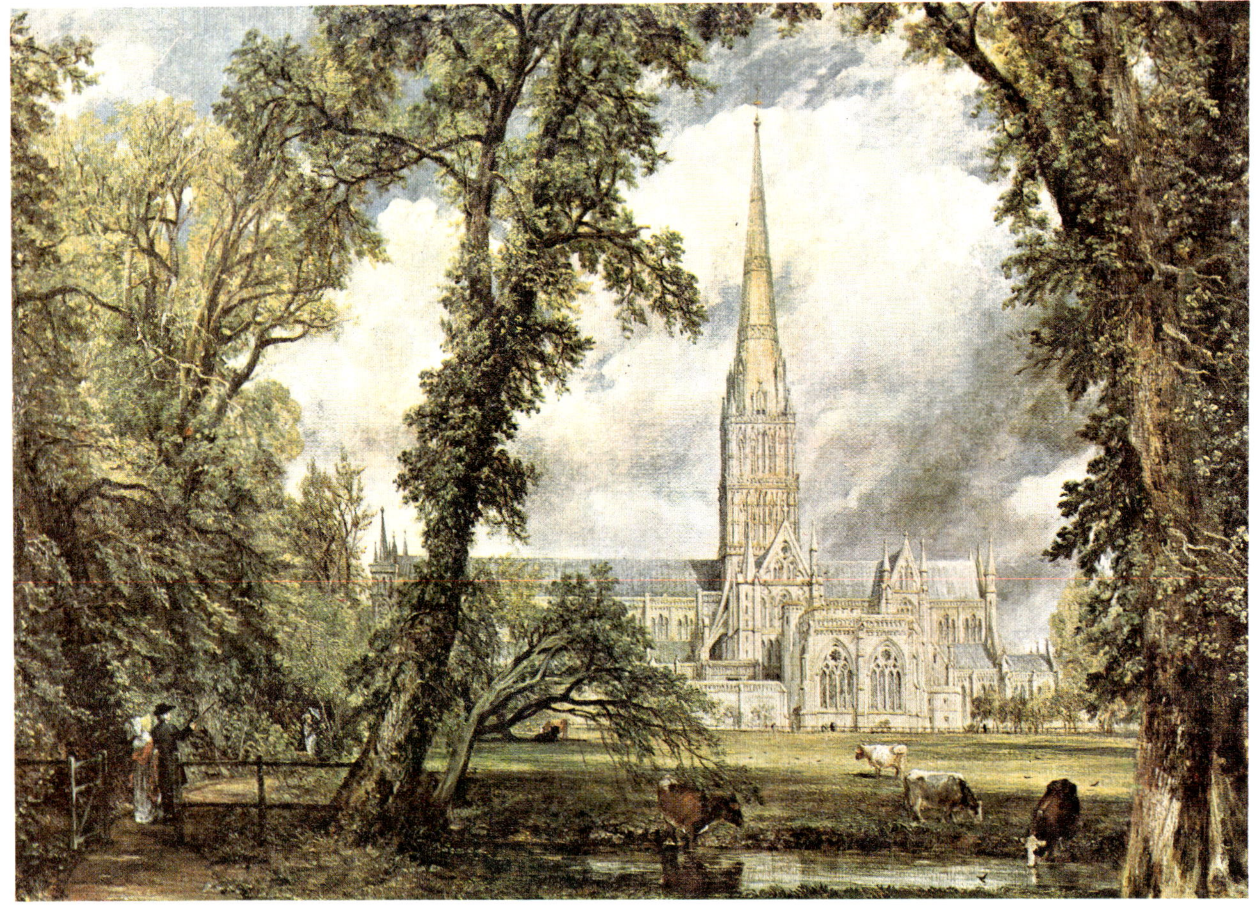

Salisbury Cathedral from the Bishop's Grounds, 1823. Victoria and Albert Museum, London.
Bishop Fisher—who commissioned this painting—and his wife are seen passing through the gate between their garden and the meadow in front of the cathedral. The cows seem to be feeling the heat and either rest in the shade or drink from the stream. It seems however that the fine weather will shortly change for dark clouds are looming. The contrast they make with the light stone and grey roofs of the cathedral framed by the trees forms a striking composition.

to claim her and her doctor advised sea air. Since one of their sons was at school nearby, the Constables began to visit Brighton frequently. Everywhere he went, Constable took his sketchbook, and he made many studies of the downs and the sea-shore, though he disliked the popular resort and wrote to Fisher that its 'din and tumult' compared unfavourably with 'dear old Osmington'.

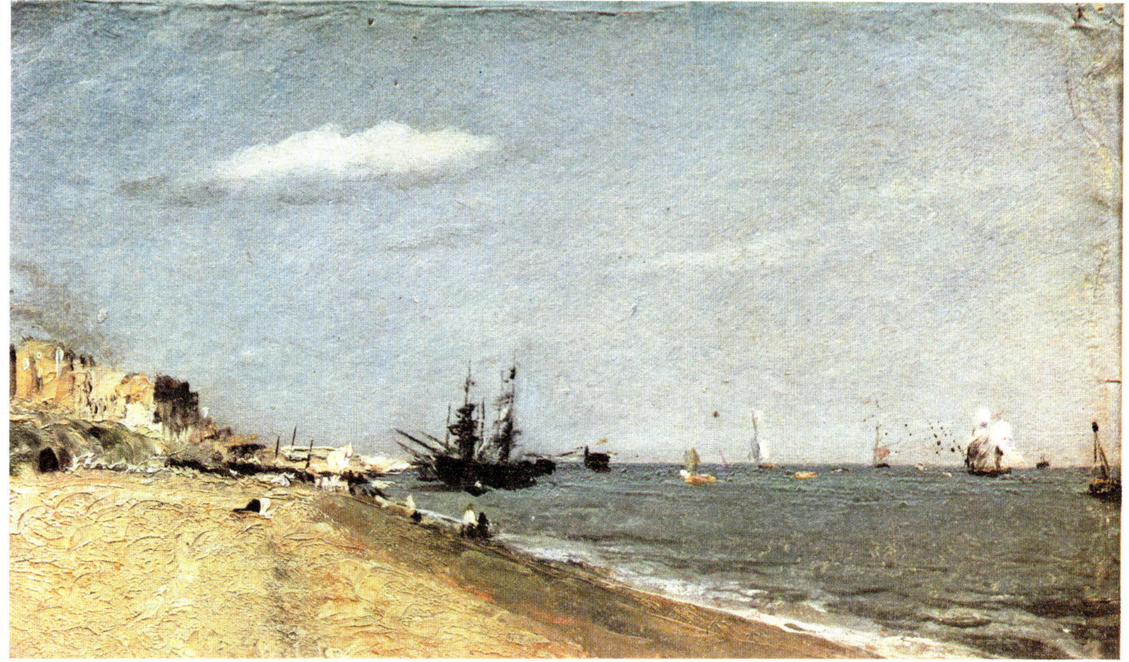

Brighton Beach with Colliers, 1824. Victoria and Albert Museum, London.

One of these sketches is *Brighton Beach with Colliers* (p. 17). It is in oil on paper and measures only $5\frac{7}{8}$ by $9\frac{3}{4}$ inches. Despite the small size of the work the greater part of it depicts the clear emptiness of a hazy summer sky. Many of his sketches are accompanied by notes about the day's weather and on the reverse of this one is written '3d tide receeding left the beach wet—Head of the Chain Pier Beach Brighton July 19 Evg., 1824—Very lovely Evening—looking Eastward—cliffs & light off a dark grey effect—background—very white and golden light'.

In 1825 he completed *The Leaping Horse* (p. 18) after many experimental sketches to find the perfect viewpoint and composition. He had told Fisher that he did not consider himself at work unless he was before a six-foot canvas, and the one he used for this painting measures 4 feet 8 inches by 6 feet $1\frac{3}{4}$ inches.

In 1826 Constable completed *The Cornfield* (p. 19) which with *The Haywain* is probably the painting for which he is best remembered. Though the picture was not sold in the artist's lifetime, it was bought by his friends after his death and presented to the nation in his memory.

In this year he also completed *A Boat Passing a Lock* (p. 19) for a client, though it seems not to have been exhibited until 1829, when Constable bought it back to present to the Royal Academy as his Diploma work. The lock is the one shown in *Flatford Mill* (p. 12), and the foot bridge beyond is seen in *A View on the Stour near Dedham* (p. 15). *Cont. p.20*

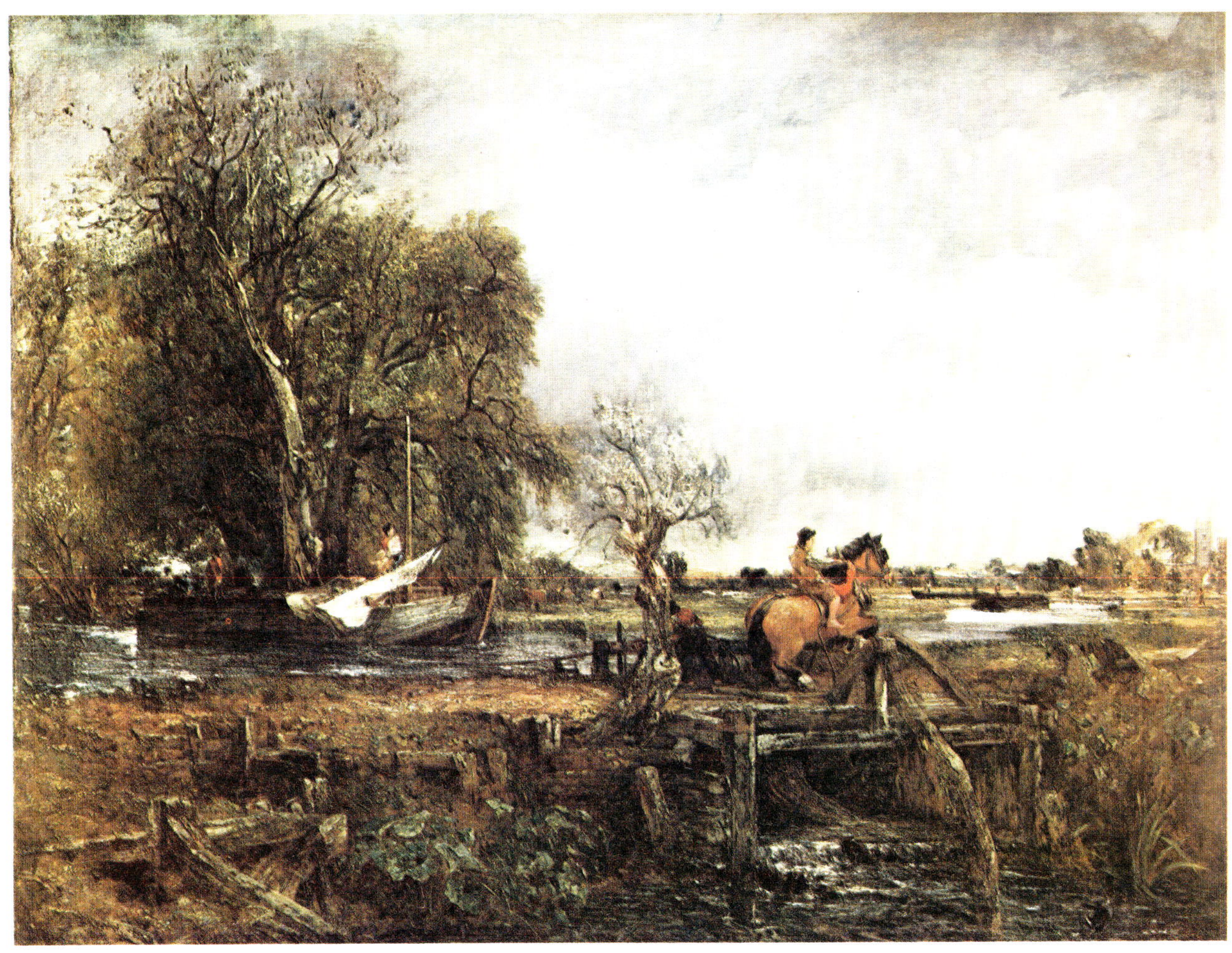

The Leaping Horse, 1825. Royal Academy, London.
The scene is once again beside the River Stour near Dedham and the tower of the church is visible in the distance. In the foreground a barge horse is seen jumping a rail put on top of a sluice gate to prevent cattle straying along the towpath. The barge drifts by the far bank and the tow rope, temporarily slackened, trails in the water. At the bottom of the painting water can be seen escaping from the main channel through the sluice where a moorhen, startled by the noise, hurries to the safety of the rushes.

Constable's great interest in natural effects of clouds and sky is shown in the large area devoted to them here. The confidence and accuracy with which the action of the heavy horse jumping is painted shows the artist's familiarity with the scene, which he must have witnessed many times. This painting shows how Constable made use of carefully chosen everyday events to give life to his paintings. The memorable or unique themes commonly chosen by other artists of the day would have been at variance with the idyllic country life he strove to convey.

The Cornfield, 1826. National Gallery, London.
This painting shows the lane leading from East Bergholt to Dedham which Constable would have walked along each day on his way to school. It is the height of summer with sunlit trees on each side and in the distance beyond the cornfield a river wandering through the lush valley. The church and river in the background are, however, imaginary.

On the far side of the field two men can be seen harvesting the ripe corn, while in the foreground a shepherd boy thirsty from the heat is lying drinking from a pool of clear water. This distracts the attention of his dog, which allows his sheep to wander off down the lane. The scene has been noticed by the farmer watching from his field of corn. As the gate has been taken off its hinges, he is moving towards the entrance to the field in case the sheep show interest in his corn.

Outside the gate is the plough the farmer will use to prepare the ground for the following crop, when the harvest is over. A donkey, apparently unattended, feeds from a hedge with her foal beside her.

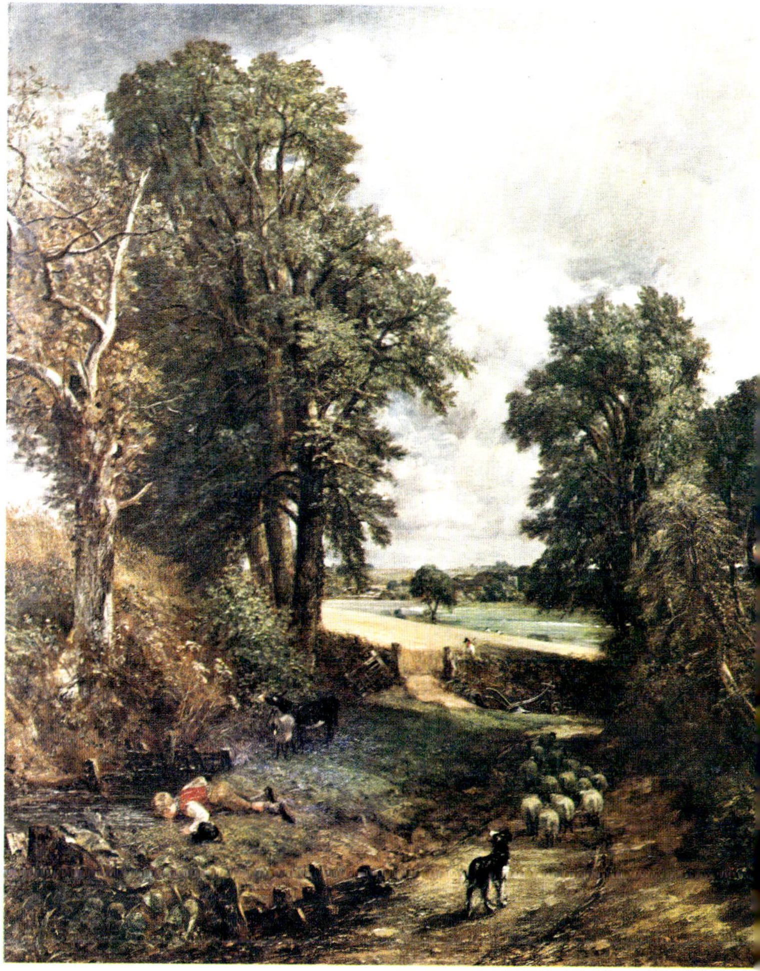

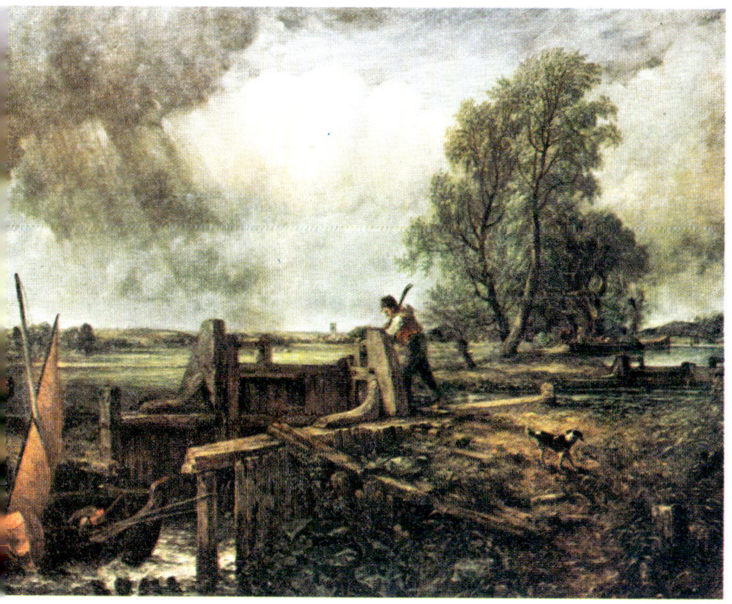

A Boat Passing a Lock, 1826. Royal Academy of Arts, London.
A barge can be seen straining at its mooring as water pours from the sluice being opened by the bargeman to lower the water level in the lock.

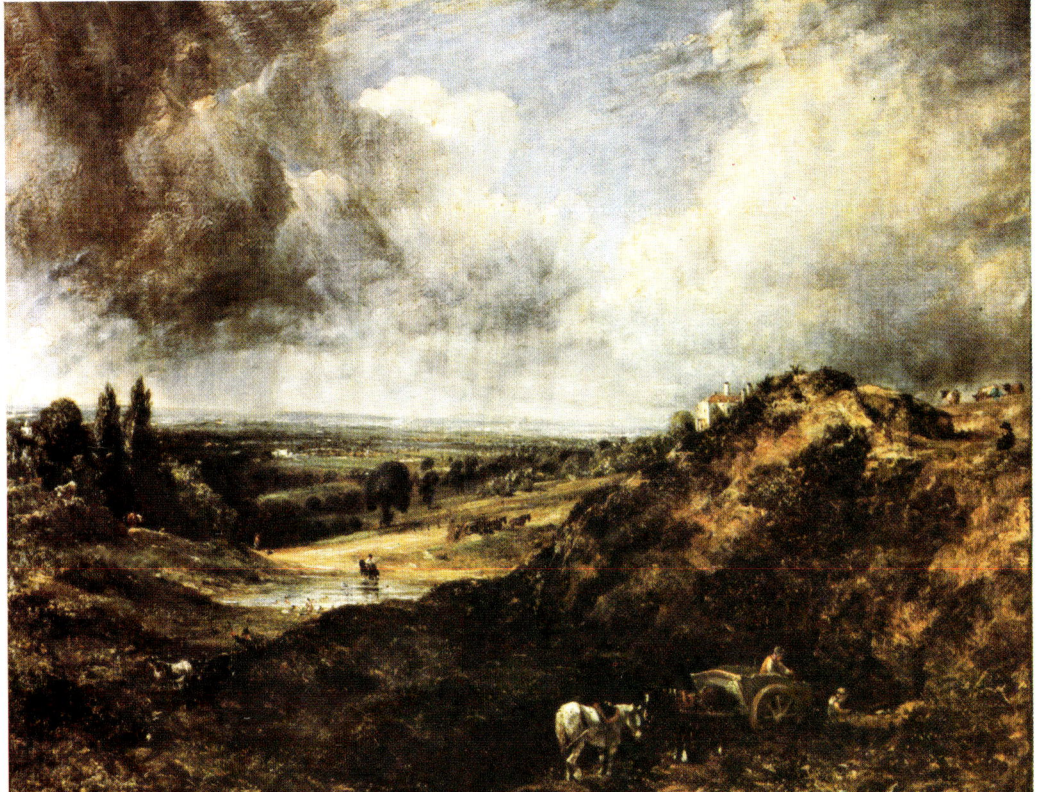

Branch Hill Pond, Hampstead Heath, 1828. Victoria and Albert Museum, London. Constable often visited Hampstead for the sake of his wife's health and they went to live there in 1827. He painted a number of versions of this view.

Owing to a disagreement with Arrowsmith, who later became bankrupt, Constable was now no longer selling paintings to the French dealers. This would have meant a serious loss of income had it not been for the increasing interest in his paintings in England. In 1827, indeed, *The Times* review of *The Chain Pier, Brighton*, his major work that year, refers to him as 'unquestionably the first landscape painter of the day' though this picture also found no buyer to ease Constable's continuing financial problems.

The Constable family moved in 1827 from central London to Hampstead where the better air had been recommended for Maria's poor health. He told Fisher that the house commanded one of the finest views in Europe, stretching from Westminster to Gravesend with the dome of St. Paul's rising in the centre of the city. The view of *Branch Hill Pond, Hampstead Heath* (p. 20) was one of his exhibits at the Royal Academy in 1828 and its dark clouds and stormy atmosphere reflect his concern over his wife's illness.

Maria had given birth to their seventh child, a son, in January 1828, and in March her father had died, leaving them £20,000, a much greater sum than expected, but though Constable's financial worries were over, his life was to be a sad one from now on. With his wife seriously ill at home and his brother Abram unwell at Bergholt, his travelling and family responsibilities left little time for painting. Despite moves to Putney, then Brighton and back to Hampstead, Maria's health continued to decline and on November 23rd she died at the age of 41.

Constable now left Hampstead with his seven children, the youngest not a year old, and returned to their former home at Charlotte Street, engaging a housekeeper to look after his family. After Maria's death he wrote 'Every gleam of sunshine is blighted for me' and he never recovered the joy of life his earlier work so clearly shows. His pictures now bore heavy layers of paint with dark stormy skies and sinister beams of light. *Fording the River, Showery Weather* (p. 21), the full-sized sketch for his finished picture *Salisbury Cathedral from the Meadows*, shown

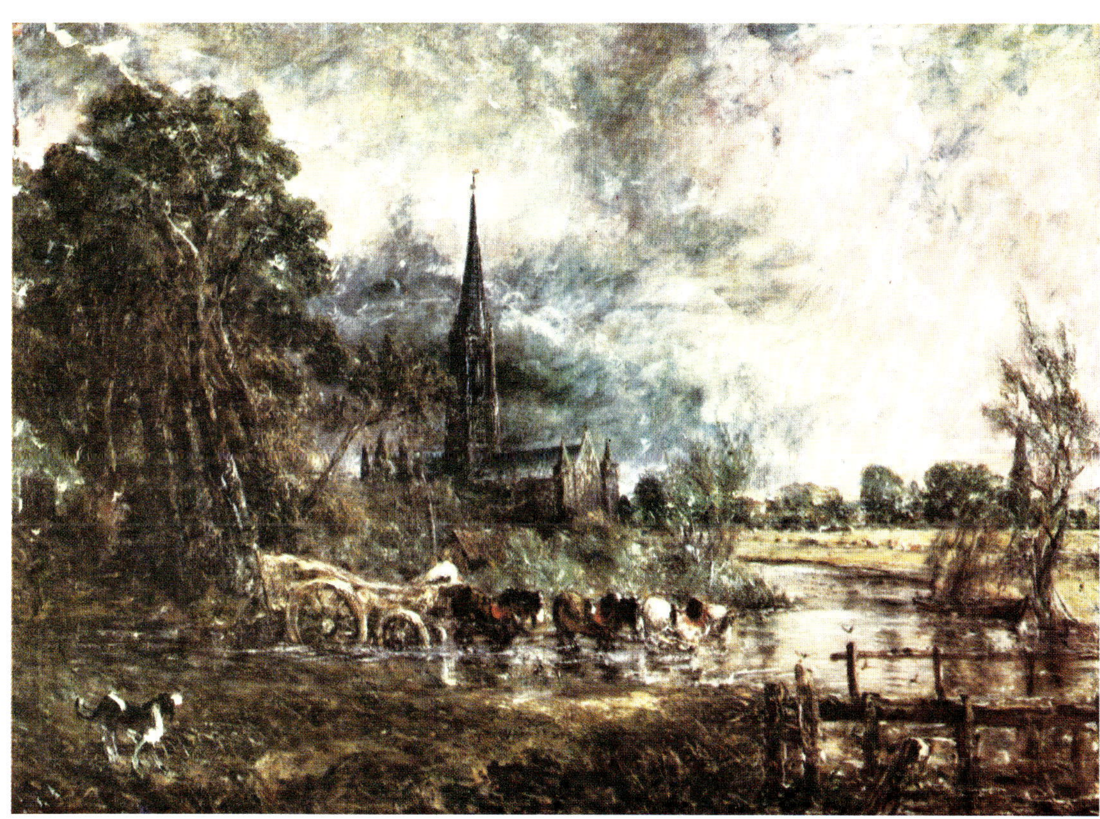

Fording the River, Showery Weather, 1829. Guildhall Art Gallery, City of London.

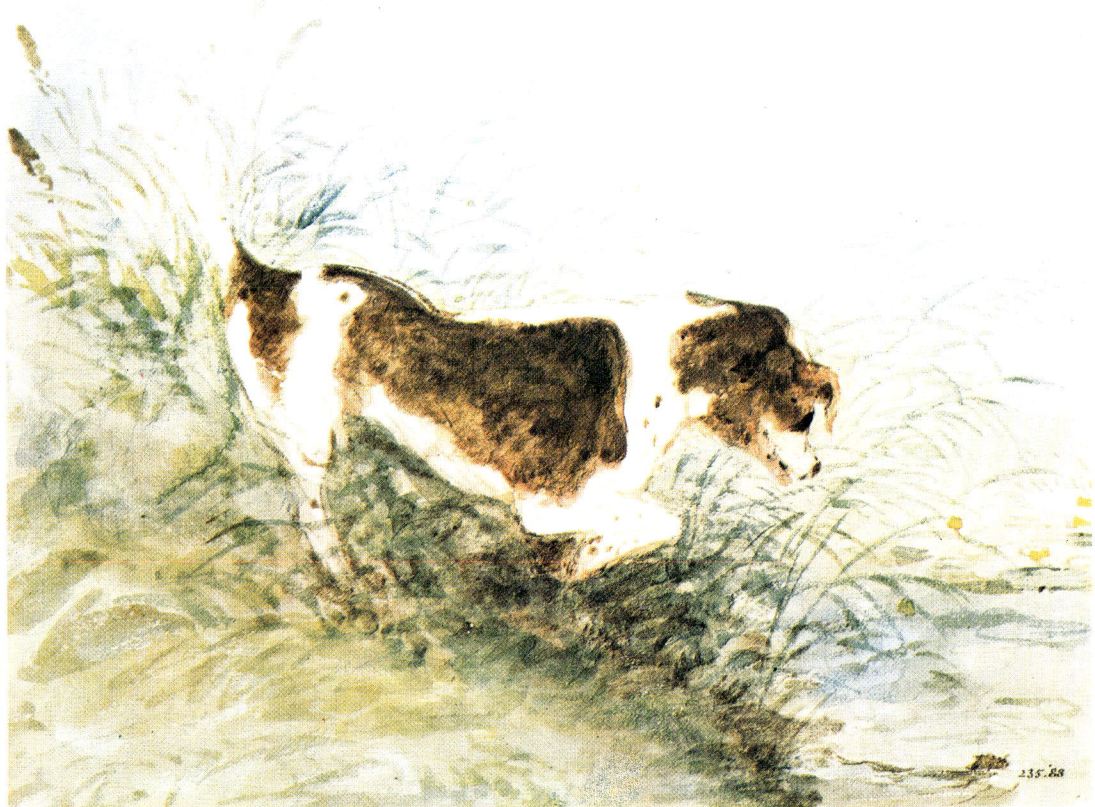

A Dog Watching a Rat in the Water at Dedham, 1831. Victoria and Albert Museum, London.

at the Royal Academy in 1831, was conceived in 1829 on one of his last visits to Fisher and is indicative of his distress at this time, especially when compared with his earlier painting of the cathedral (p. 16).

More sorrows were to come, for his children suffered from much illness and his life-long friend and supporter, John Fisher, died whilst visiting Boulogne with his wife in August 1832. A further blow fell in November of the same year when his assistant and friend John Dunthorne also died.

In 1829 Constable, now fifty-three years old, had at last been elected a full member of The Royal Academy though he felt that the honour had come too late and the President, Sir Thomas Lawrence, had scarcely been welcoming, saying that he was lucky to have been elected at all!

His paintings were now largely of scenes from his earlier life—frequently, of course, the countryside about his Suffolk birthplace, which he still visited with his children. The two watercolour sketches on pages 22 and 23 show that the country life had not lost its appeal. His Academy pictures in 1833 included *Cottage in a Cornfield* and in 1835 *The Valley Farm* and *The Glebe Farm*, all new treatments of earlier themes.

In 1832, however, he showed at the Academy his largest painting yet, *Whitehall Stairs: The Opening of Waterloo Bridge*, 7 feet $2\frac{1}{2}$ inches long. Constable, having watched the Prince Regent opening the new bridge in 1817 on the second anniversary of the battle, had begun to plan a picture two years later, and the intervening years saw many preparatory sketches and experimental studies. No other picture gave him so much trouble.

His principal new painting in the 1836 Academy was a watercolour, *Stonehenge* (p. 24). He wrote on the mount 'The mysterious monument of Stonehenge, standing remote on a bare and boundless heath, as much unconnected with the events of past ages as it is with the uses of the present, carries you back beyond all historical records into the obscurity of a totally unknown period'. The rainbows, so frequent in his last works, and the hare, bounding away to the left, symbolise the transience of life he must so strongly have felt.

Constable's last painting was a scene of *Arundel Mill and Castle* for which he had made sketches while staying with a friend there in 1834 and 1835. The picture was to be hung at the Royal Academy of 1837.

On March 31st of that year, having spent the day in London working on the painting, he went to bed as usual but awoke in the night in considerable pain

A Suffolk Child, c.1835. Victoria and Albert Museum, London.

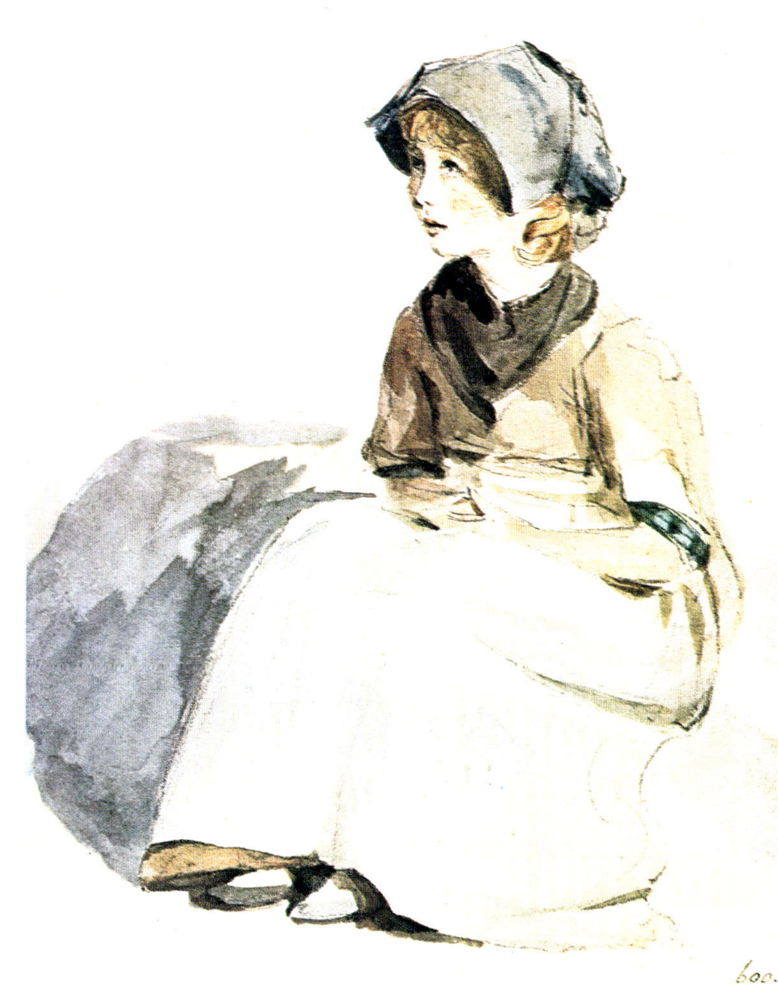

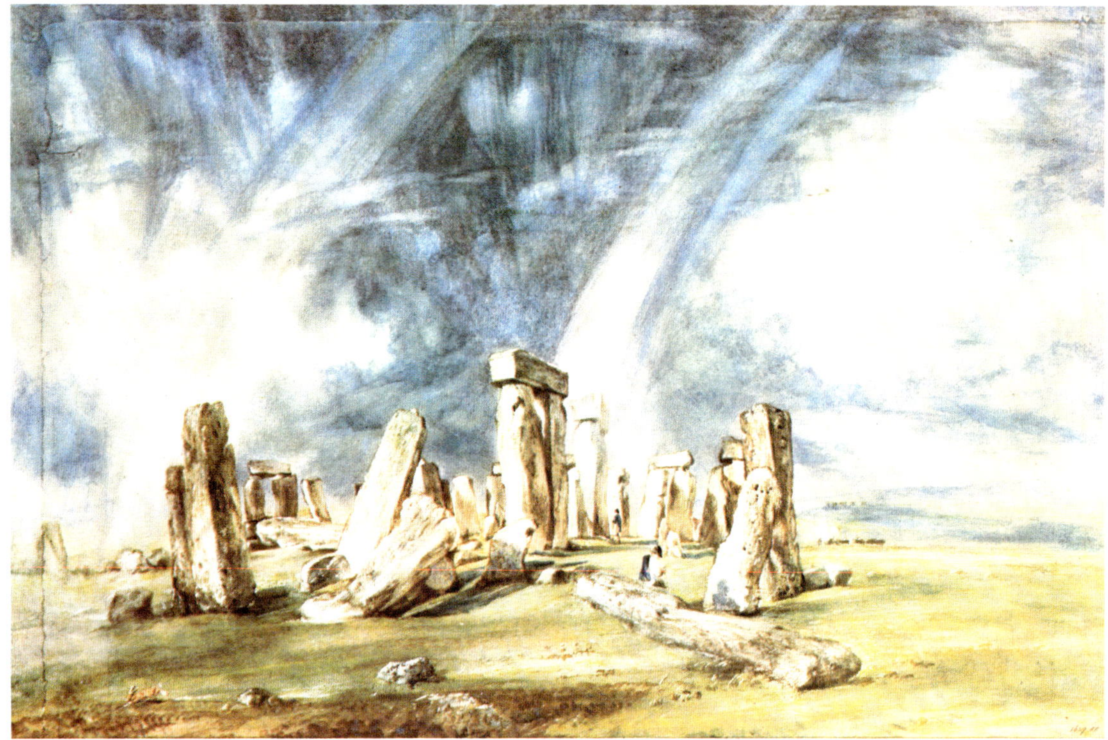

Stonehenge, 1836. Victoria and Albert Museum, London.

and died within an hour. A post-mortem was held, but failed to reveal the cause of his death. He was buried at Hampstead in the vault which had contained the remains of Maria since her death nine years before.

John Constable inherited the grand style of the classic French and Dutch landscape painters and applied his new approach to the representation of colour and atmosphere. With his contemporary, Turner, he was the first artist to express the importance of the changing effects of weather and daylight on the appearance of a country scene.

This turning point in the development of European art was not generally recognised in England until long after his death. In France, however, his influence was much felt. The painters of the Barbizon and Impressionist schools learnt from him the importance of painting out-of-doors in understanding the effects of varying weathers and times of day, and Troyon and Monet, pioneers of their respective movements, both made careful studies of his work.

He may truly be said to have achieved his stated ambition to 'preserve God's Almighty daylight which is enjoyed by all mankind'.